MARTIN**TAYLOR**

WALKINGBASSLINES FOR**JAZZ**GUITAR

Learn To Masterfully Combine Jazz Guitar Chords With Walking Basslines

MARTIN**TAYLOR**

FUNDAMENTAL**CHANGES**

Martin Taylor Walking Basslines For Jazz Guitar

Learn To Masterfully Combine Jazz Guitar Chords With Walking Basslines

Published by **www.fundamental-changes.com**

ISBN 978-1-78933-029-8

www.fundamental-changes.com

Twitter: **@guitar_joseph**

Over 10,000 fans on Facebook: **FundamentalChangesInGuitar**

Instagram: **FundamentalChanges**

For over 350 Free Guitar Lessons with Videos Check Out

www.fundamental-changes.com

With special thanks to Pete Sklaroff for his invaluable help in putting this book together.

Cover Image Copyright: Robert Burns, used by permission

Contents

Contents

About the Authors

Dr Martin Taylor MBE is a virtuoso guitarist, composer, educator and musical innovator.

Acoustic Guitar magazine has called him, "THE acoustic guitarist of his generation." Chet Atkins said that Martin is, "One of the greatest and most impressive guitarists in the world," and Pat Metheny commented that, "Martin Taylor is one of the most awesome solo guitar players in the history of the instrument."

Widely considered to be the world's foremost exponent of solo jazz and fingerstyle guitar playing, Martin possesses an inimitable style that has earned him global acclaim from fellow musicians, fans and critics alike. He dazzles audiences with a signature style which artfully combines his virtuosity, emotion and humour with a strong, engaging stage presence.

Taylor has enjoyed a remarkable musical career spanning five decades, with more than 100 recordings to his credit. Completely self-taught, beginning at the early age of 4, he has pioneered a unique way of approaching solo jazz guitar that he now breaks down into seven distinct stages in order to teach others.

Joseph Alexander is one of the most prolific writers of modern guitar tuition methods.

He has sold over 400,000 books that have educated and inspired a generation of upcoming musicians. His uncomplicated tuition style is based around breaking down the barriers between theory and performance, and making music accessible to all.

Educated at London's Guitar Institute and Leeds College of Music, where he earned a degree in Jazz Studies, Joseph has taught thousands of students and written over 40 books on playing the guitar.

He is the managing director of *Fundamental Changes Ltd.*, a publishing company whose sole purpose is to create the highest quality music tuition books and pay excellent royalties to writers and musicians.

Fundamental Changes has published over 120 music tuition books and is currently accepting submissions from prospective authors and teachers of all instruments. Get in touch via **webcontact@fundamental-changes.com** if you'd like to work with us on a project.

6

Introduction

One of the things I'm most often asked is how to play walking basslines on guitar. Between my private students and at every guitar retreat I teach, inevitably someone will ask me how to combine chords with walking basslines while keeping a tight jazz groove and driving the song forward.

It's a great question. Being able to play chords and basslines at the same time is the ultimate accompanist's skill for a jazz guitarist, whether you're jamming in a guitar duo, working with a singer, or even playing in a bigger band with a piano. In fact, my chord and bassline approach sits at the core of my playing, so mastering it will give you a deep insight into my chord melody style.

This book will teach my technique of combining chords and walking basslines from the ground up, starting with the most important chord shapes and fingerings, right through to constructing basslines and mastering the jazz swing feel.

I'll teach you how to introduce syncopation, mimic jazz drummers, add the bass player's iconic "skip" and give you plenty other tricks of the trade. All this will help turn you into a groovy accompanist that other musicians will be dying to work with.

At the heart of all groove is the skill of *listening*. It's very important that you check out a number of great bass players, so you can hear how these lines should actually sound. Everything we do in this style is about imitating the bass player, so if you've not heard the musicians listed below, it will be worth your while to seek them out and spend some time listening before diving into Chapter One.

Some of my favourite bass players include:

• Niels-Henning Ørsted Pedersen

• Ray Brown

• Oscar Pettiford

• Jaco Pastorius

Listen to these incredible musicians and focus on their groove and note placement to capture their feel. If you like, you can try to copy their feel by playing along on a muted bass string.

Before we get going, I want to give you one final piece of advice: *Please* don't play walking basslines when you're playing with an actual bass player. You'll create loads of clashes and just get in their way. Playing walking basslines is the bass player's job, after all, so only use these wonderful techniques when there's no bass player available. Your band will thank you!

Now that's out of the way, let's dive into Chapter One and look at some of the most appropriate chord shapes to use when playing walking bass. Pay attention to the fingerings as they might not be quite what you're used to.

Get the Audio

The audio files for this book are available to download for free from **www.fundamental-changes.com.** The link is in the top right-hand corner. Click on the "Guitar" link then simply select this book title from the drop-down menu and follow the instructions to get the audio.

We recommend that you download the files directly to your computer, not to your tablet, and extract them there before adding them to your media library. You can then put them onto your tablet, iPod or burn them to CD. On the download page there are instructions and we also provide technical support via the contact form.

For over 350 Free Guitar Lessons with Videos Check out:

www.fundamental-changes.com

Twitter: **@guitar_joseph**

Over 10,000 fans on Facebook: **FundamentalChangesInGuitar**

Instagram: **FundamentalChanges**

Get the Video

As a special bonus to buyers of this book, Martin Taylor has two videos that explain every key element of his walking bass and chords technique, that are not available anywhere else. Follow this link to view/download the content:

https://fundamental-changes.teachable.com/p/martin-taylor-walking-bass-for-jazz-guitar

Or use the short link:

http://geni.us/walkingbassvideo

If you type above link into a browser, please note that there is no "www."

You can also scan the QR code below to view the videos on your smartphone:

Chapter One – Essential Chord Voicings

While most jazz guitarists know some big and impressive guitar chords with terrifying names, it's most common (and more effective) to use very small fragments of chords when learning to play chords in tandem with a walking bassline.

These fragments are called "root and guide tone" voicings, as they contain just the root of the chord, normally played on the 6th or 5th string, and the *guide tones* of the chord (the 3rd and 7th) which are played on two of the middle strings of the guitar. The 3rd and 7th are the notes that best define the sound of a chord and indicate whether it is a major 7th (Maj7), minor 7th (m7), or dominant 7th (7).

Throughout this book you won't see a single note played on the high E string. We're only concerned with the bass notes and middle chord voices, and you'll be amazed how intricate and grooving we can make just these small fragments sound when they're combined with a jazz walking bass.

As you probably know, there are some important chord changes in jazz that crop up time and time again, and we are going to use one of these as the framework to hang all our walking bass ideas on. The progression is a I VI II V (pronounced One Six Two Five) sequence in the key of G Major. You may know this sequence as a *rhythm changes* progression, as it forms the backbone of the song *I Got Rhythm*, and many other standard jazz tunes, such as *Oleo* and *Anthropology*.

In the key of G,

Chord I is GMaj7

Chord VI is Em7

Chord II is Am7

Chord V is D7

We'll look at how these chords can be altered later, but for now let's begin by learning these chords as *guide tone* voicings in their most basic form on the neck. Pay attention to the fingerings; a couple may feel unnatural at first, but there is a reason for playing them like this that will become apparent. Make sure the notes marked with an X are muted.

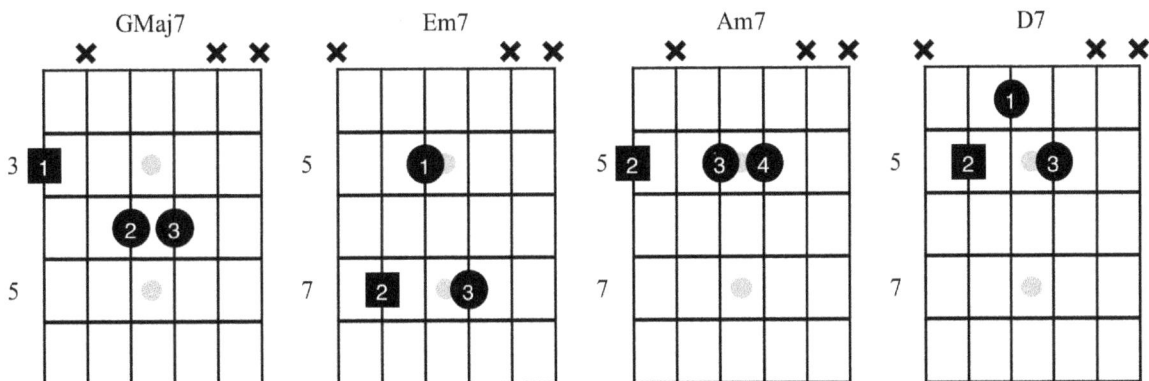

Let's play these chords as a simple jazz progression. Use your fingers and be sure to mute the unwanted strings.

Example 1a:

These chords are *diatonic* to the key of G Major. This means that every note in every chord is contained in the G Major scale. However, jazz musicians like to mix things up a bit and often they will play a G7 instead of a GMaj7, an E7 instead of the Em7, or an A7 instead of the Am7.

In fact, pretty much the only chord that's set in stone is the D7, and sometimes you'll see substitutions for that too. We'll come back to substitutions later in the book. For now, try playing the I VI II V sequence using the following chords.

Example 1b:

When you can play Example 1a and Example 1b fluently, try combining them and getting the sounds of the different possibilities into your head. For example, you could try the following sequence:

Example 1c:

Try looping the I VI II V sequence repeatedly and using different chord *qualities* each time around.

Next, I'm going to teach you an important chord *substitution*. Instead of the GMaj7 (or G7) chord, we will play a Bm7 chord. This substitution sounds great because Bm7 contains the guide tone (3rd and 7th) notes of GMaj7 and adds an extra note.

Compare the chord tones of GMaj7 and Bm7:

Chord	1	3	5	7
GMaj7	G	B	D	F#
Bm7	B	D	F#	A

When we play Bm7 instead of GMaj7, the only difference is that we introduce the note A. Normally, if a bassist or piano player is playing the original root note G, we hear the A as a beautifully rich note added to the harmony. Don't worry though, this substitution works beautifully whether there is a bass player or not!

Try playing through the following progression using this voicing of the Bm7 chord. The first time through I play a G7. The second time through I play Bm7 instead of the G7. Loop this sequence until you're confident before moving on.

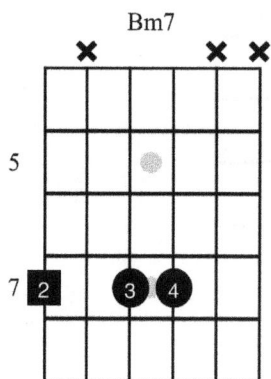

Bm7

Example 1d:

Using a Bm7 (chord III) instead of chord I is a very common substitution in jazz and the two chords are completely interchangable. You can use either and it won't affect the soloist or a singer.

We'll get to the walking bass section soon, I promise! But first we need to open up the neck a little more and learn some different ways to play around the I VI II V chord sequence in different areas of the fretboard.

How about starting up high on the neck and descending from a G7 at the 10th fret?

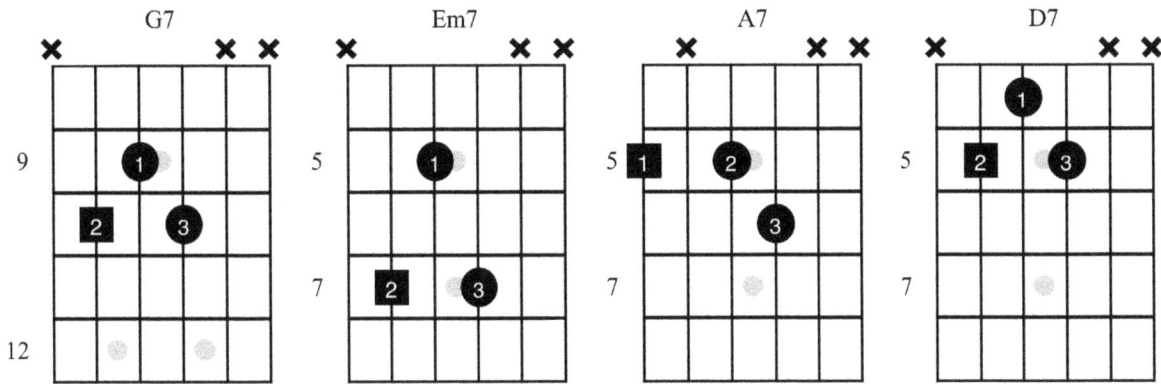

Example 1e:

We could also descend from the lower G7 and play an E7 using some open strings.

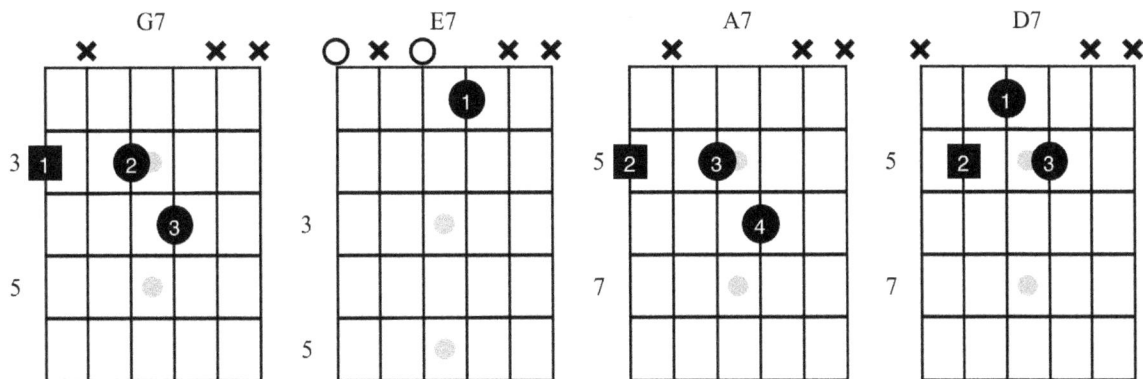

Example 1f:

We can relocate the Am7 and the D7 at the top of the neck. This works great if we begin with the Bm7 substitution.

Example 1g:

Of course, we could begin with the G7 too!

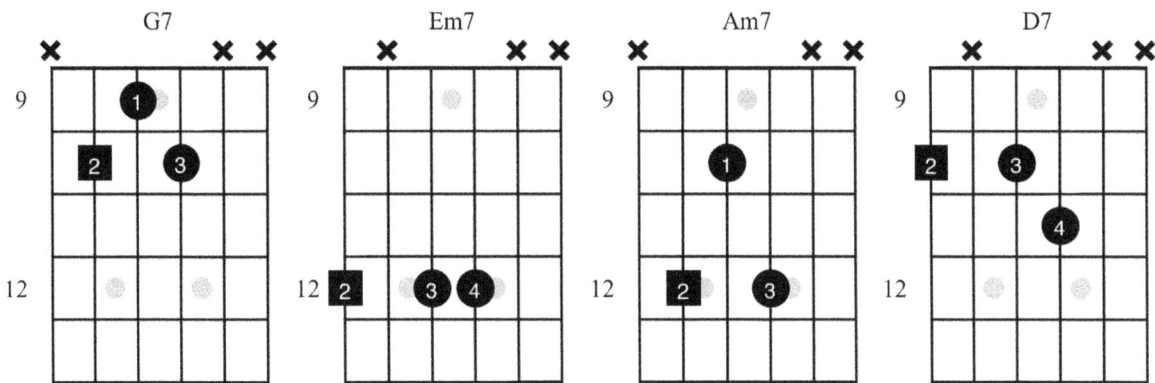

G7 Em7 Am7 D7

Example 1h:

G7   Em7   Am7   D7   G7   Em7   Am7   D7

The most important thing to do is experiment and have fun with these progressions. In later chapters we will add walking basslines and more rhythmic interest, but for now explore this chord sequence in G Major and discover how it feels to play all the substitutions we've covered.

You can play:

Chord I	GMaj7	G7	Bm7
Chord VI	Em7	E7	
Chord II	Am7	A7	
Chord V	D7	(Top tip: Try Ab7 too!)	

Before we move on, I'd like you to learn this sequence in another key. This will help develop your understanding of the neck and make it easier to transpose these ideas quickly when working with a singer or brass section.

Begin by learning the I VI II V progression in the common jazz key of F.

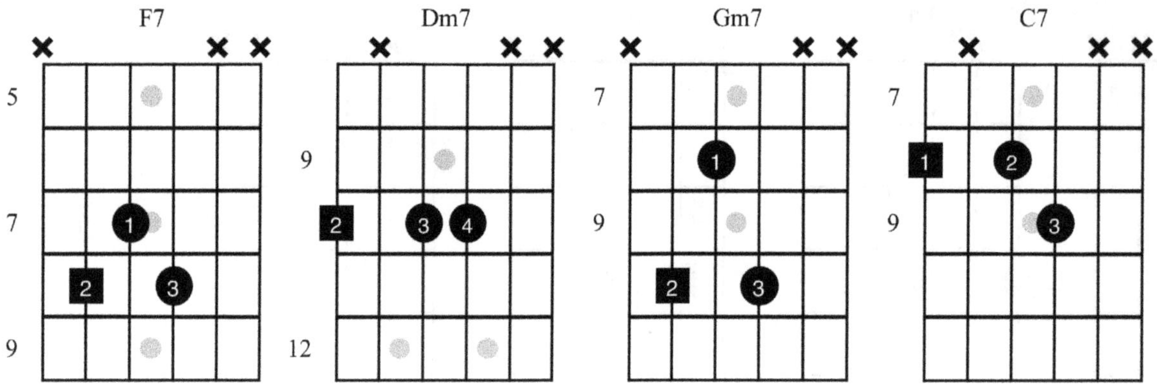
F7
5
7
9
Dm7
9
12
Gm7
7
9
C7
7
9

Example 1i:

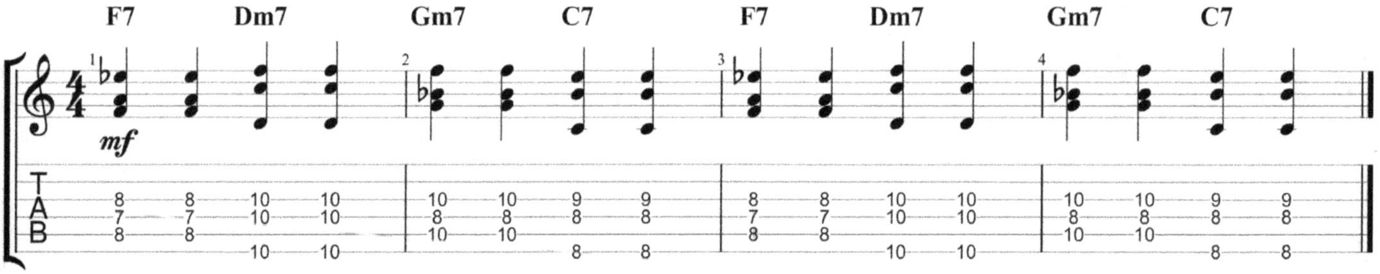
F7
Dm7
Gm7
C7
F7
Dm7
Gm7
C7
4/4
mf
1
2
3
4
T
A
B

Chapter Two – Simple Walking Bass

Now we know how to voice the important chords and substitutions in the I VI II V progression, let's take a look at how to build a simple bassline. The first step is to play only the root of each chord. Even though you already know where the root notes are from Chapter One, play through the following exercises using your first finger to play each bass note.

Play the root twice on each chord, but pay attention to how I accent each note. The first note is longer and the second note is slightly *staccato* (cut off). Listen to the audio and try to copy my feel.

Example 2a:

Now, let's play the same thing, but starting from the Bm (the III chord) we used as a substitution in the previous chapter

Example 2b:

When you've got that down, link up the previous two examples.

Example 2c:

Finally, take some time to explore the other positions of the neck for both the I VI II V and III VI II V sequence. Here's one way you could play through the changes, but you should spend time exploring the neck yourself.

Example 2d:

OK, now that we know where the important bass notes are, how do we begin to walk? Well, it's easier than you think!

To create a solid walking bassline all we need to do is add a *chromatic approach* note either above or below the target bass note. In other words, instead of playing two root notes on each chord, we replace the second note with a chromatic approach note a semitone above or below the *following* chord.

When written down this sounds a little more complicated than it is, so let's look at the first two chords, G and E.

When we played two notes on each chord, we had the following:

Example 2e:

Replace the second G with the note a semitone above the E (F).

Example 2f:

Let's repeat this process on every chord in the bar so that each bass note is approached from a semitone above. Use your first finger to play every note. It might feel a bit basic, but at this stage I want you to learn the sound, feel and location of the notes and not trip over your fingers.

Example 2g:

Can you hear how suddenly we've become bass players?! The root notes of the chords are all on the strong beats of the bar (beats 1 and 3) and the chromatic approach notes are all on the weak beats of the bar (beats 2 and 4) This means that not only have we created *movement*, we've created a *tension* that *resolves* when we move to the targeted root note.

These chromatic movements won't get in the way of any other instruments (apart from another guitarist or a bassist who is playing a walking bassline) because they all occur at weak points in the bar and resolve strongly to root notes.

It's the same process when we want to move to the root note from a semitone below. Begin on G then approach the E from the chromatic note below (D#). Use your first finger to play each note in the following example.

Example 2h:

Approaching the root from a semitone below sounds just as strong as approaching it from above. Musically, it has the same effect, as once again the tension on the weak beat resolves to the root note on the strong beat.

Now begin on chord III (Bm) and play though the sequence adding a chromatic approach note from above.

Example 2i:

Repeat this exercise using chromatic approach notes from below each chord.

Example 2j:

When you're confident, link the I VI II V and III VI II V sequences together using chromatic approach notes from above.

Example 2k:

Repeat this example, but with chromatics approaching each chord from below.

Example 2l:

After you've spent some time on the previous two examples, it's time for you to get creative and mix up the chromatic approach notes. Combine chromatic approach notes from both above and below and play whatever you feel. I've given you one example below, but consider this a creative task – find as many ways as you can to navigate the progression. Stick to using one finger and try to create a musical feel that really sounds like a bass player.

Example 2m:

When you're confident creating a walking bassline, explore different positions of the neck. Here's one idea played in a low register.

Example 2n:

Now play high up on the guitar.

Example 2o:

It's worth spending some time here, as really knowing your territory on the guitar neck will help you massively when we combine walking basslines with chords in the next chapter.

Before we move on, here's a creative challenge:

Set your metronome to 60 beats per minute (bpm) and see how long you can walk for on the I VI II V III VI II V sequence. Your priority is to always place a root note on beats 1 and 3. If you make a mistake, just keep going and try not to lose your place.

Always record your practice sessions and review your playing 24-hours later. Pay attention to your rhythm (are you playing in time?) and see if there are any places where you consistently struggle or lose your place in the progression. If there are, isolate those parts and work on the movements individually.

As your confidence grows, apply all the techniques in this chapter to the key of F. The chords you need are shown at the end of Chapter One.

In Chapter Three, we will reintroduce the chords and have some fun combining them with basslines.

Chapter Three – Chords and Harmonised Basslines

In the previous two chapters we learnt how to play chord voicings for the I VI II V progression and how to build a chromatic bassline. In this chapter we will combine these two skills and also *harmonise* the chromatic approach notes to create a self-contained chord and bassline structure.

As you saw in Chapter One, there are various *qualities* we can play for each chord, so to keep things simple we will stick with the following chords to begin with.

At the end of the chapter I will show you a few important variations and how to approach them musically.

The first step is to *harmonise* (add chords to) the chromatic notes we added to the basslines in Chapter Two. This sounds complicated, but actually it's very simple.

You'll remember that all we did to create our walking bassline was to add a chromatic note either a semitone above or below the target note. To harmonise these chromatic notes, we simply play a chord that has the same quality as the target chord.

For example,

- If we approach Em7 from a semitone above (F) we play an Fm7 chord.

- If we approach A7 from a semitone above (Bb) we play Bb7

- If we approach D7 from a semitone *below* (C#) we play C#7

- If we approach G7 from a semitone above (A#) we play A#7

We will learn some lovely variations later, but this approach is incredibly solid and will always sound good.

Let's take a look at this in action on the I VI II V sequence.

In the following example, I play each chord in the progression and create a bassline by approaching each one by a semitone from above. I then harmonise the approach note using a chord of the same quality as the target chord.

Example 3a:

Now repeat the process, but this time approach each chord from a semitone from below.

Example 3b:

This time, let's explore the III VI II V sequence, first by approaching chromatically from above.

Example 3c:

And now chromatically from below.

Example 3d:

When you've wrapped your fingers around all that, try combining both progressions. In the next example I've shown each chord approached from below, but you should also play it approaching each chord by a semitone above.

Example 3e:

Just to get you started, here's an example that combines chromatic approach notes from both above and below.

Example 3f:

Before moving on to the second part of this chapter, explore the other regions of the neck that were covered in Chapter Two. It should be an easy job to apply the techniques in the previous six examples to other areas of the fretboard. Also, apply everything to the chord sequence in the key of F Major.

Now you're confident playing the chords and bassline around the neck, let's examine how to approach different chord qualities. As you might expect, the informal "rule" is that the approach chord should have the same quality as the target chord, but there are a few exceptions that sound great, so let's take a look at these now.

So far we've been playing a G7 as chord I. However, in quite a few tunes, the I chord needs to be played as a GMaj7. When this happens, I still *like* to approach it using a dominant 7 chord from above. In other words, the chord that precedes the GMaj7 is an Ab7. It is played in the following way.

Example 3g:

This "rule" also applies when you approach the GMaj7 from below – an F#7 sounds great.

Example 3h:

While this is my preference, playing an AbMaj7 chord before the GMaj7 still works well, so trust your ears and choose your favourite! You'll often find that they are interchangeable.

When we use the Bm7 (chord III) substitution, I'll also normally approach that from above using a dominant 7 chord, i.e., C7 in this instance.

Example 3i:

However, when I play a chromatic chord below the Bm7, I'll often play a minor 7 chord – in this case, an A#m7.

Example 3j:

These are two of the most common variations I use, but you will find your own with practice.

Before moving on, here are a couple of longer sequences that combine the I VI II V and II VI II V chord progressions using the approaches in this chapter. Learn them carefully before improvising your own ideas.

Example 3k:

Example 3l:

Finally, expand these sequences to other areas of the guitar neck. Here's one idea in the higher register.

Example 3m:

As always, use a metronome and record your playing. Listen back to yourself 24-hours later and pay careful attention to your rhythm and groove. When you're ready, learn everything in the key of F too!

OK, we've got a lot of the groundwork done now. We have learnt the chords, the bassline ideas and harmonised the chromatic approach notes. In the next chapter we're going to take a more detailed look at rhythm and syncopation. This is the stage where your musical feel will develop quickly and you'll really start to hear the bass and chords become separate voices.

Chapter Four – Syncopation and Separation

So far, we've studied the nuts and bolts of combining walking bass and chords on the guitar, and in this chapter we're going to learn how to "separate" the parts and make it sound like there are two instruments playing together. This is where the magic happens and your jazz feel can really develop.

Our aim here is to allow the steady 1/4 note walking bass pattern continue, while the target chords are moved and played on the off-beats of beats 1 and 3. For the moment, we will omit the chords played on the chromatic approach notes, but add them back in later for some variation and interest.

Let's begin by getting the fundamental rhythm of the two parts working together.

Play the bass note of the G7 chord on beat one, and with a slow and lazy swing, play the rest of the chord (the two notes on the middle strings) on the off-beat, before quickly jumping up to the F on beat 2, which is the chromatic approach note to the Em7 on beat 3.

Repeat the chord rhythm before playing the Bb chromatic approach note to A7 on beat 4. Repeat the rhythm and feel with the A7 and D7 chords in bar two. Approach each chord from a semitone above.

In the following examples, keep the chord stab short and staccato.

Example 4a:

Try playing the same rhythm and approach every chord with a chromatic step from below.

Example 4b:

Repeat the previous idea using the Bm7 in the sequence. First, play chromatic approaches from above.

Example 4c:

Now try the same progression approaching from the chromatic note below the chord.

Example 4d:

Finally, play the full I VI II V / III VI II V progression and combine chromatic approaches from both above and below. Here's one route around the changes, but you should be able to come up with many more!

Example 4e:

As I'm sure can hear, the bass and chord parts are starting to sound like two different instruments. This is perfect and exactly what we're aiming for.

The next stage is to try to accentuate that difference by playing both parts at different volumes. We want the bassline to be loud and proud, and the chord stabs to be quieter and less obvious.

In the next example all the chords are approached from a semitone above, and I've really exaggerated the volume difference between the bassline and the chords. It's a bit over the top, and I'd never play like this on a gig, but it's done deliberately to cause you to think hard about your volume levels. Separating the *voices* in this way is quite an advanced skill, and one that takes practice to make it sound natural, so to begin with, exaggerating the dynamics will help to build the independence between your thumb and fingers.

Example 4f:

Working on the "volume controls" between your thumb and fingers is a real challenge for most students at first, but it gets easier with time. A little trick I like to teach is to get my students to play the bassline once through loudly *without* the chords, and on the repeat to add the chords back in as quietly as possible. It takes a lot of practice, but this additional dynamic adds great depth to the musicality of the guitar part. Try this on the I VI II V sequence.

Example 4g:

I will reiterate, this is an advanced skill, so keep coming back to the previous two exercises and practise them often.

Until now, all the chord stabs have been played *staccato* (short and detached). However, it's possible to let the occasional chord ring out, as a contrast to the stabs, by leaving the fingers on the higher strings while you play the next note of the bassline.

This is one of those things that's easier to hear than it is to explain, so listen carefully to the audio track before playing through Example 4h. On the I VI II V progression, play chords I and II staccato, letting chords VI and V ring for one beat. The trick is to leave the fingers playing the chord in position for as long as possible, while the spare finger plays the bassline. It's important to keep the bassline simple at first, so always approach the target chord by a semitone from above.

Example 4h:

These types of variations keep the texture of the rhythm guitar parts interesting and break up any monotony.

Another way to add interest is to move the position of the chord stabs in the beat. Until now, we've played each chord on the "and" of beats one and three, but with a bit of practice we can move them on to the 1/16th note divisions of the beat.

To develop this rhythmic feel, forget about the whole chord sequence for a moment and just hold down a G7. Play the bass note with your thumb and quickly play the rest of the chord immediately afterwards. Let the chord notes ring for two beats and repeat this sequence four times.

Example 4i:

When you're confident with this rhythm, apply it to the four chords in the I VI II V sequence.

Example 4j:

Now add the 1/4 note walking bass back in. I've notated the bass approaching from above, but when you're ready you can begin to improvise your own basslines.

Example 4k:

Finally, this 1/16th note stab can be played at any point in the bar and works beautifully on any of the harmonised chromatic bass notes. In the following example, I play all the chords with the normal 1/8th note syncopated chords, but on the chromatic bass notes *preceding* the A7 and the G7, I use the 1/16th-note rhythm to harmonise those approach notes.

Example 4l:

Try doing the same thing with the 1/16th note stab before the Em7 chord.

Example 4m:

We've now developed three chord rhythms we can use when playing a walking bass.

a) The first is to simply play straight, un-syncopated chords on every beat of the bar.

b) We can play 1/4 note bass notes with a syncopated chord on the 1/8th note off-beats.

c) We can also play the 1/16th note stab I taught you in the previous few examples.

There's also a "secret option D", however, which is to play the 1/4 note bassline without any chords at all. This provides a steady pulse for a singer / soloist to work with, while thinning out the texture of the music, should it be required.

The most common approach is option b, but by combining the four techniques it's easy to create an interesting, grooving part that adds to the music and doesn't become monotonous. When you combine these approaches with the different ranges on the guitar (playing up high or down low), and add in some substitutions, (like playing Bm7 instead of the G7), there are hundreds of creative options for you to explore while improvising a walking bassline.

The following example gives you 16 bars of me playing through the I VI II V sequence, putting together all the harmonic, rhythmic and substitution ideas we've learnt so far. I've added a couple of new ones, so keep your ears open! Learn this example note for note and use it as a basis for your own exploration.

Example 4n:

When you're getting to grips with Example 4n, get out the metronome and really concentrate on your rhythm. Set the metronome to click at about 80bpm and focus on playing all the bass notes on the clicks. When that's solid, add a bit of "snap" to the chords by digging in a little harder with your fingers.

One useful metronome technique is to half the speed of the click and "hear" it as beats 2 and 4. You must fill in beats 1 and 3 yourself. Set the metronome to 40bpm and play at the same speed as you did when it was set to 80bpm. You should hear every chromatic bass note fall on the click and the root notes fall in the gaps. Listen carefully to Example 4o and play along to develop the feel.

Example 4o:

There's been a lot to learn in this chapter, but we've now covered the main components of an effective walking bassline on guitar. The key here is for you to practise these ideas as much as possible. Your bass should be loud and confident, and your chords should be quieter and snappy. Work towards the point where you have total control over the rhythms, chords, syncopations and volume you play.

It's OK to plan what you're going to play at first, as this will help you to develop discipline and control, but soon all the techniques will begin to combine naturally and you'll start to play what you hear.

Keep listening to bass players too, because this will quickly help to develop your feel.

In the next chapter, we'll look at how we can vary the dynamics of the guitar part by using a pick.

Chapter Five – Imitating Drums with the Pick

In this chapter I'll teach you something that will add a whole new feel and dimension to your walking bass parts.

Even with all the variations to the walking bass we've looked at in the previous few chapters, you may find that the music sometimes calls for another colour.

One of my favourite things to do is imitate a drummer by using my guitar pick instead of my fingers to create a more percussive effect on the strings. By holding the pick in a particular way, and playing with a relaxed, laid back rhythm, it's possible to create the effect of a drummer's brushes on the snare drum while still playing the walking bassline.

When you've learnt this technique, it'll sound like you're playing guitar, bass and drums all at the same time! As you can imagine, that's a great skill for an accompanist and it will turn you into an extremely versatile rhythm guitar player.

The trick to imitating the "swish" of a drummer's brushes it to *angle* the pick as it crosses the strings. I like to turn the pick so that its leading edge is pointing up to my left shoulder. In this position, instead of the flat edge of the pick striking the strings, the curved edge is the part that makes contact. Other guitar players turn the pick so that the leading edge points down towards their knee, so experiment with what feels best for you.

Let's begin by learning the strumming pattern and feel you'll use to mimic the drummer's brushes. With the pick angled as described above, play two 1/4 note down strums followed by a quick, light, soft up-strum on the second off-beat.

Begin by fingering a Bm7 chord, but don't press the strings all the way down to the fret wire. When you strum, be careful not to hit any open strings and you will create a deadened percussive effect. This rhythmic technique is one reason why I tend to use these little chord fragments and avoid full barre chords. Fingering chords in this way really helps to stop unwanted strings from ringing and gives me a great deal of control over my dynamics. Don't forget that everything is played on the bottom four strings!

Play a Bm7 chord and listen to the scratchy feel on the upstroke. You don't want to hear any of the muted strings individually. Instead, aim for a brush-like effect, so that the strings blur into one as the edge of the pick glides across them. Play softly until you can hear that swish and try to match my feel on the audio track.

Example 5a:

Now try this rhythm on a properly fretted Bm7. The chords on each bar should be strong, but release the pressure between each strum to make them staccato. Also release the pressure on the upstroke to play the muted scratch. Play softly!

Example 5b:

When you can match the feel on the audio track, apply the rhythm to the III VI II V progression.

Example 5c:

Now let's add the walking bass back in, along with the harmonised chords on the chromatic approach notes. Keep those up-strums going on the off-beats.

Example 5d:

When you have that down, play the rhythm throughout the full sequence as shown below.

Example 5e:

As you gain confidence, start to bring in some of the substitutions we've covered in earlier chapters. The following four examples apply the brush rhythm to other ideas we've covered.

Example 5f:

Example 5g:

Example 5h:

Example 5i:

Now string some of these examples together into one longer piece.

Example 5j:

Finally, before we move on, transpose the chord sequence into the key of F Major to test yourself. I've shown it in its basic form here, but you should apply all the substitutions you've studied in the key of G Major.

Example 5k:

This has been a short chapter, but it's an important one. The brushes feel is essential to master, as this adds a distinctive rhythmic element to your playing that other instruments can't copy. When you've practised this feel, you'll sound like a guitarist, drummer and bass player all at once!

In the next chapter, we'll look at how to add some rhythmic interest to the bassline.

Chapter Six – Walking Bass Variations

We've now covered many of the elements of playing a walking bassline on guitar, and in this chapter we'll take a look at some of the ideas that will help you to get more creative with your rhythm and texture. We'll explore how to play walking bass with a "two" feel, how to play up at the dusty end of the fretboard, how to add a little bit of melody, and how to play the minimum of chords while still laying down the harmony of the tune.

Some of these ideas are less tangible than others and will develop more with practice. They are often about feel, which is something I can't teach in this book. The secret to developing great feel is to listen to your favourite musicians (especially bass players in this instance) and play with other people as much as possible.

We will begin with one of the most tangible elements of texture: playing in twos.

Until now, we have been walking with four even bass notes in each bar, but now we will vary that and use a different rhythm to accentuate the root notes on beats 1 and 3.

The trick is to delay the chromatic approach note until *just before* the target note. The listener begins to hear the bassline phrased in twos and it's almost like we've created a half-time feel. It's a great effect and all we need to do to achieve it is delay the chromatic approach note.

Listen to the audio track before playing Example 6a and you'll get the idea immediately. Begin with chromatic approach notes from above each chord and only play the bassline for now. We'll add the chords back in later.

Example 6a:

Now apply the same rhythm to the III VI II V sequence and use a chromatic approach from below.

Example 6b:

Let's link those two sequences together and harmonise every bass note, including the chromatic approaches.

Example 6c:

This time, don't harmonise the approach note, and syncopate the chord so that it falls on the off-beat. This creates a great feel and is definitive of the style.

Example 6d:

Now you've got the two feel under your belt, it's time to combine it with the four-to-the-bar walking bassline. For now, forget about chords and practise moving between twos and fours. There are infinite ways you can do this, but here are a couple of examples to get you going.

Example 6e:

The previous example gave you a predictable place to move from twos to fours, but I like to do it in the middle of the sequence too. Here's an idea that moves to fours on the Am7.

Example 6f:

When you're confident with this feel, add the syncopated chords back in. Here's another way to move from twos to fours, now with the chords played on the off-beats.

Example 6g:

Of course, there are unlimited ways to combine chords on the beat, chords off the beat, playing in fours, playing in two, and playing unaccompanied basslines. It's up to you to get creative and try out as many permutations as you can. The following idea will get you started. It's an eight-bar phrase that mixes up all the approaches listed above. Use it as the basis for your own exploration and see how many ideas you can come up with. Set a metronome and focus on your groove.

Example 6h:

High Range Basslines

Every so often, it's great to explore the dusty end of the fretboard, so let's have a look at some ideas that work above the 12th fret. Of course, these ideas may be difficult to play depending on what type of guitar you own, but they should be doable on most jazz boxes.

One word of warning though: don't use these ideas all the time. You've got to pick your moment, because the high pitched "bassline" could start to interfere with what a singer or soloist is doing.

The following ideas are all based on the same I VI II V / III VI II V chord progression, but are played high up on the neck. They shouldn't need too much explanation by now, as they use the same concepts we've discussed in earlier chapters, so just learn them and explore each approach to make it your own.

The first idea starts at the 10th fret and gradually descends the neck.

Example 6i:

The next idea begins from the B (chord III) at the 14th fret and descends to the G at the 12th fret.

Example 6j:

This route around the changes begins at the 15th fret and targets the E at the 19th fret. It might be easier to play it as just a bassline to begin with and add chords later.

Example 6k:

Root and Tenths

For a change of texture, it's possible to move away from playing full chords and instead play the root and 10th (3rd) of a chord. For a comprehensive guide to this technique, check out my book *Beyond Chord Melody* where I get deep into building melodies with these shapes. For now, here's a quick overview.

Instead of going deep into the theory, I think it's best to just show you a few practical examples of where I add some melody on the second string.

The first idea begins on the Bm7 chord and as the bass note moves to F (chromatically above the target of E), I add a G melody note on the 8th fret on the second string. This melody ascends a semitone to G# as the bass note descends to E. The two notes together form an E7 chord. I then repeat the process after approaching the A7 in bar two from a chromatic note above.

Pay particular attention to this example as it is a common feature of my playing and, while the fingering is a little awkward, this contrary motion is quite captivating for your audience.

Example 6l:

The following example is easier and played once again beginning on a Bm chord, this time at the top of the neck. Notice how I only play two notes on each chord. This tiny change helps to accent the melody and give the harmony part more space.

Example 6m:

The final example in 10ths outlines the chords GMaj7, Em7, Am7 and D7, with the first three chords approached from a semitone below and all played with a root on the fifth string. The D7 is approached by a semitone above and is played off the sixth string. As you can hear, we don't need to play complex ideas to give the chords room to breathe and create additional interest.

Example 6n:

This root and tenth approach is a huge part of my chord melody playing style, so I do encourage you to check out my book *Beyond Chord Melody* which explains it in detail. However, in the context of playing a walking bassline, these voicings are yet another way you can break up the monotony of the guitar part.

Before moving on, try the following suggestion.

Plan out your entire walking bass part covering 32 or even 64 bars. Use some tablature and jot down the root notes you'll use and get your "geographical" positions fixed on the guitar. Then, above each four- or eight-bar phrase, write down which texture or rhythm you're going to use. See if you can build a part from an unaccompanied bassline, right up to a busy bass and melody part, and then bring it back down again.

The textures and rhythms we have covered are:

- Walking bass only

- Every bass note harmonised on the beat

- Only target chords harmonised on the beat with a walking bassline

- Every bass note with a syncopated chord

- Only target chords harmonised with syncopated chords and a walking bassline

- Harmonising with just roots and 10ths

- Playing in fours

- Playing in twos

- Playing with a pick to imitate brushes on the drums

- Loud Bass / Quiet Chords

- Quiet Bass / Loud Chords

Many of the items on the above list can be combined, so you should never be short of ideas. Grab a blank piece of paper and compose your walking bass part, learn it, then compose another one. Gradually, all of the ideas will become internalised and you will be able to improvise these parts unconsciously.

We're going to add a few more ideas into the mix in the next chapter, so make sure you're solid on these ones before moving on.

Chapter Seven – Jazz Skips

In this chapter, I'm going to teach you two beautiful rhythmic variations that I use when playing walking bass: jazz bass skips and picking thumb flicks.

Jazz bass skips are the one rhythmic idea I'm *always* asked about when I teach walking basslines. They are a specific triplet rhythm idea that upright bass players often add to their lines to create great groove and interest. They sound *fantastic* and, while most people think they're some sort of industry secret, the skip is actually quite simple.

The skip is a triplet *inflection* you can bring in to break up the regularity of the 1/4 note bassline. Most people think I'm doing something very clever with my note choice here, but as you will see, it's all a clever illusion! However, while the technique is uncomplicated, as with everything in music, this is all about feel. You *must* go and listen to jazz bass players and immerse yourself in the music to get that groove under your skin.

To perform a jazz bass skip, I simply add a *muted* triplet on the notes of the chord. In other words, I pick the bass note with my thumb normally, then relax the pressure with my fingers on the middle strings to mute the notes and pick them with the index and ring fingers of my picking hand.

As with learning any new skill, let's isolate the movement before reintroducing it into the turnaround chord progression.

Begin by holding down a Bm7 chord. Fret the root note normally and let the other fingers just touch the third and fourth strings to mute them. As this chord is played at the 7th fret, you might find that you accidentally create a couple of harmonic notes when you're trying to mute the strings. If this happens you'll need to press very slightly harder.

Play a triplet with your thumb, index and middle fingers as shown below. Repeat the triplet four times to complete a whole bar. Listen carefully – the bass note should sound normally and the middle strings should be muted. Adjust your hand if you start hearing harmonics. Loop this until you get it right.

Example 7a:

When you've got that down, let's learn how to move to the E7 chord via a chromatic F7. For now, the F7 and E7 chord ring for a full beat. Repeat this until it's comfortable.

Example 7b:

Next, play the same thing, but add the skip to the E7 chord and continue to play Bb7 immediately after.

Example 7c:

Now you're ready to take that pattern through the whole turnaround sequence. Play a muted triplet skip on each of the target chords, and play the approach chords as sustained 1/4 notes.

Example 7d:

The previous few examples will help you master the feel of the triplet skip. Of course, we are overplaying it at the moment, to really internalise the technique. Soon we'll make these ideas sounds much more tasteful, but first let's try placing the skip in some different places.

First however, I want to introduce you to a picking technique I use when the music is too fast for the "Thumb and muted middle string" muted skips we used in the previous four examples. I frequently play the triplet as "thumb middle-strings thumb". The first bass note of the triplet is played normally, then the middle strings and final (thumbed) bass note are muted. We will use this technique for the next few examples and you will find it easier to play at speed.

In the previous example, we played the skip on the target chords. Let's now place it on the chromatic approach chords. Again, use fully held chords (no syncopation), but this time begin from G7.

Example 7e:

When you've got that, repeat the previous idea and reintroduce the syncopation so that all the target chords are playing on the off-beats.

Example 7f:

Finally, let's reverse that, so the skips are played on the target chords and the approach chords are syncopated. Play through the sequence from Bm7, and notice that this idea may feel a little more technically awkward. Ensure every bass note is consistent and has an even volume – it's easy to accidentally mute too many notes.

Example 7g:

You wouldn't necessarily play the ideas in Example 7g too often, but it's a bit of a finger twister that is designed help you to focus on the clarity of the bassline. Take it slowly and pay attention.

It's also possible to play two skips in a row. In the following example, I add the skips to the Am7 and Eb7 chords before landing on the D7 chord. Practise this with and without syncopated chords on the off-beats.

Example 7h:

By now, you're starting to get the idea. Skips can be added at any point in the sequence to break up the rhythmic monotony of the bassline and draw in the audience. They also help to inject some energy into the rhythm part and will help to inspire the soloist.

As with most things, less is more, so don't overplay these ideas. They'll be much more effective if the listener isn't expecting them.

The following three ideas add skips to different chord textures to show you some different ways of introducing them. The first is introduced while playing an unaccompanied bassline.

Example 7i:

Here's an idea that's 90% bassline. I play a skip late in the sequence on the Am7 and follow it with a single syncopated chord on the D7.

This example also teaches you one final picking pattern I use to play the muted triplet skip. This time I play the first note of the triplet with my thumb, then play the second note on the muted 3rd string, and the final note on the muted 4th string. This technique is much like the way a classical guitarist would approach the technique and, when combined with the other two approaches I taught you earlier, gives you a very diverse way to approach playing walking basslines that creates a lot of subtle nuance.

Example 7j:

Finally, here's an idea that begins with un-syncopated chords until I add a skip on the Bb7. After that I play syncopated chords except for the isolated bassline on the note Eb. The skip helps to add a bit of energy and encourages the transition from 1/4 note to syncopated chords.

Example 7k:

The key with all these techniques is to simply play them for hours. You need to internalise them and develop a feel for where they should be played. Listening to great musicians is the most important thing you can do, so check out the recommended listening at the end of this book. The ideas sound fairly pedestrian when you play them straight, but really come alive when you add a deep jazz swing.

Here's a 16-bar example of me playing these ideas with a strong swing. Try to copy my feel as much as possible.

Example 7l:

In the next section, we'll look at a technique that seems to be unique to my style and is an effective way to add more percussive rhythm and melody to walking basslines.

Chapter Eight – Thumb Flicks

If you've played any fingerstyle or classical guitar, you'll probably have been told that you shouldn't ever play an upstroke with the picking thumb. Well, I'm going to teach you how to break that rule right now! I've been doing these thumb flicks for years and it's become an integral part of my sound.

All it involves is a little upward flick of the thumb onto a muted string to create a percussive effect, just before landing on a properly fretted note. It helps a lot if you have a bit of thumb nail, as you'll be able to dig into the strings a little more and create a real "snap" sound.

To learn this technique, listen to Example 8a before playing it. Play the G at the 10th fret and the F at the 8th fret normally, but before playing the E, relax the fingers of the fretting hand to mute the 8th fret, and flick your thumbnail upwards into the 5th string.

This works better if your picking fingers are pointing slightly into the guitar, like a classical guitar player. If you have a flat wrist, like a rock guitarist you may struggle a bit.

Example 8a:

Now add the flick after all three of the notes.

Example 8b:

Expand the exercise and play the thumb flick before every bass note in the sequence. Don't add chords just yet, stick to the solo bassline.

Example 8c:

Before moving on, try the exercise again, but this time only play the flick after a target chord tone. i.e., after G, E, A then D.

Example 8d:

You'll notice that if you need to change string from the fifth to the sixth after playing a flick, it can be a bit of a challenge. The answer is to flick your thumb far enough so that it actually crosses the sixth string to leave you in position to play the bass note with a down pick. It also helps to keep your thumb very loose.

To help relax your thumb, place the fingertips of your picking hand on the higher strings, and see how fast you can "tickle" the sixth string with the nail of your thumb. The more you relax, the faster and louder you'll be able to play.

Now you've got the hang of the flick, let's add the chords back in. In the following example I play straight chords (no syncopation) on the G E A and D, but notice that I don't harmonise each approach note and follow it with a thumb flick, just before landing on the target chord.

Example 8e:

Example 8f is broadly similar, but now I syncopate some of the chords while keeping the thumb flicks on unaccompanied bass notes.

Example 8f:

G7 E7 Am7 D7 Bm7 E7 Am7 D7

Like jazz skips, it's easy to overplay thumb flicks when you first start, but it's a tricky little thing to introduce so a bit of overplaying is probably a good thing when you first learn it. As you've discovered, there are many routes around the chord changes and many different textures you can use, so think about all the different rhythms we've covered and go back through the previous chapters to apply the occasional thumb flick where you think it's appropriate.

Just as we performed a triplet skip with the fingers in the previous chapter, we can also play it using the thumb. It feels a bit awkward at first and it's important to get the "picking direction" correct. After careful analysis, I've discovered that I nearly always play the triplet with the sequence "down up down" and play another down pick to land on the beat of the following bass note.

This is easier to show in a notated example, so pay careful attention to the picking directions below and listen closely to the feel of the audio track.

Example 8g:

It's important that you always play the note on the beat with a down pick, so even if the picking suggestion above doesn't work for you, make sure you land on a down stroke when you come out of the triplet.

Try adding the triplet thumb skip to the notes E and D in the I VI II V progression. Pay attention to your picking.

Example 8h:

An advanced idea you might like to try is to combine the thumb flick with the triplet skip in the picking fingers from the previous chapter. Here are three ways you can approach this to get you started.

Example 8i:

Example 8j:

Example 8k:

There are many different ways in which you can place these rhythmic ideas, so it's important to get creative. I like to be very logical when I'm playing, so I'll cycle through where I place the triplet skips and flicks. For example, I might first play a skip on chord I and work on that for 5 minutes. Then I'll place the skip on chords I and VI and work on that. Next, I'll place a skip only on chord VI, before adding a flick before chord I.

You get the idea!

You don't need to work through every permutation, otherwise you'd spend a lifetime on this, but what you'll find is that after a few hours of focused practice, you'll simply be able to play what you hear. This is the goal for all musicians, but it does take some serious "wood-shedding"!

In the following chapter, we'll look at some new bassline patterns we can use to add a different dynamic and feel to the music.

Chapter Nine – Decorated Basslines

Until now, we've approached every target note by step in 1/4 notes, either from a semitone above or below.

In this chapter, I'll show you some patterns you can use to break up the 1/4 note rhythm and approach the target bass note in new ways. These ideas are called *chromatic approach note patterns* and are commonly used by jazz players to decorate arpeggios when they solo.

We've covered the two most common chromatic approach note patterns – the semitone from above and semitone from below – but there are many more ways to target the root note. These patterns normally contain more than one approach note, so quite often they will be played in 1/16th notes and "crammed in" the available space before the target note. To execute these faster phrases, I tend to use a thumb flick.

The first chromatic approach note pattern we'll learn is to begin one tone above the target note and descend in semitones.

Example 9a:

Similarly, you could ascend using the same pattern and rhythm.

Example 9b:

And, of course, you can combine both directions.

Example 9c:

Try adding a harmonised chord to the note immediately preceding the target chord. Spend time experimenting with which notes you harmonise. You can harmonise all of them or none of them! Here's one example with ascending approach notes.

Example 9d:

Here's a different chromatic approach note pattern that begins on the tone above the target, then moves to the semitone below, before resolving to the root. Play it first without chords:

Example 9e:

Now add chords on the target notes.

Example 9f:

Let's reverse the pattern to play the semitone below the target note, before playing a tone above. Learn this as a solo bassline first.

Example 9g:

Once again, introduce the chords back into the sequence.

Example 9h:

The next "level" is to play chromatic approach notes in constant 1/8th notes, and there are a couple of important patterns you should know.

The first is "tone above, semitone above, semitone below" This is easier hear and see in notation than it is to describe, so listen to the following audio track then play along. As always, learn the bassline first before adding chords.

Example 9i:

Now add the chords in appropriate spots.

Example 9j:

The final important pattern to know is "semitone below, tone above, semitone above". Learn it on a solo bassline before adding chords.

Example 9k:

Example 9l:

As you can probably hear, these basslines get very "busy" so it's important not to use them too often. To really make them work, it's all about adding them subtly to a bassline that is walking naturally in 1/4 notes.

In the following three examples I play standard walking basslines using both syncopated and un-syncopated chords, and occasionally I add in a chromatic approach note pattern. Notice that if I play a syncopated chord, there's no time to use a 1/8th note idea.

Example 9m:

Example 9n:

Example 9o:

Spend time getting creative with these basslines and think carefully about the options available to you. You can play syncopated or off-beat chords, add skips and flicks, or any other technique we've covered in the book. Think about whether you will harmonise only the target chords, or whether you will harmonise the approach notes too.

While the faster chromatic approach note patterns are used as an effect when we play two chords in a bar, they are a great basis for forming walking basslines when we play chords for longer durations.

In the next chapter I will teach you some new approaches to use when we play walking bass on a chord that lasts for a whole bar.

Chapter Ten – Walking into the Bar

We're covered a lot of ground in the past nine chapters, from the basics of rhythm changes to some exciting rhythmic feels and chromatic ideas. Until now, everything has been based on playing when there are two chords in the bar. Well, what happens if there's only one chord in the bar and we need to walk for four beats?

In this chapter, I'm going to show you how to expand our ideas to cover any chord that lasts for four beats and show you some different ways to walk between some of the most important chord sequences in Jazz.

Let's begin with moving from chord I to chord IV – the first chord change in a blues. In the key of G, that's G7 to C7.

The good news is that everything we've covered so far works as we move between these chords, and the easiest way to begin is to add a chromatic "sidestep" idea to the G7, then approach the C7 by a chromatic approach note from above or below. You can play a similar idea when moving from C7 back to G7.

This is much easier to understand when you play it.

Example 10a:

When you're confident with this idea, harmonise both the target chords and the approach notes immediately preceding them. Use the same chord quality for the approach chord as the target chord. In the first two bars I play un-syncopated chords, but in the second two I use off-beat chords.

Example 10b:

This kind of movement is the basis of playing longer walking basslines, but of course there are almost unlimited paths we can walk between just these two chords. The key to finding these lines is to listen to great bass players and copy their pathways, but to get you started I'll show you some of my favourite movements.

Notice which bass notes get harmonised and which bass notes don't. These are by no means hard and fast rules, but they should give you a good insight into my style, and the stylistic considerations of the genre in general. Joe Pass was a master of these ideas and people often think he's playing extremely complex chords while walking. However, more often than not, he's using the same three-note voicings as me. Listen carefully to his playing and watch him on YouTube. It's quite an education.

Here are a few more ways to move from G7 to C7 and back. Memorise them and come up with your own variations.

Example 10c:

Example 10d:

Example 10e:

The next line is a common idea to use when you have two bars of G7. Notice how it moves to a Bm7 chord – an inversion of G7 at the beginning of the second bar.

Example 10f:

The following example shows how I like to substitute an F7 chord when I play two bars of C7 in a blues.

Example 10g:

Now let's take a look at some ideas I play when tackling the "slow turnaround" section of a blues. It's the same as the I VI II V sequence we've been studying for most this book, but now each chord lasts for a whole bar.

Example 10h:

Example 10i:

As you can see, there are limitless ways to move between one chord and another. What it really comes down to is keeping the target chord as your "goal". As long as you hit it on the right beat, then you won't go too far wrong. The rest is a combination of scale steps (normally taken from the tonic key), chromatic approach notes from above or below, and chromatic approach note patterns.

Some notes of the bassline are harmonised. If you're harmonising the chromatic approach note above or below the target chord, you'll usually harmonise the approach note with the same chord *quality* as the target.

When harmonising a scale step, you'll normally use the appropriate chord from the harmonised parent scale. For example, in the key of G Major, the chords are

GMaj7, Am7, Bm7, CMaj7, D7, Em7 and F#m7b5.

However, as we've seen, almost any of those chords can have their quality altered. For example, GMaj7 is often played as G7 and Am is often played as A7. Keep experimenting and listening to great jazz so that your ears begin to guide you.

The best way to learn these skills is to write out a bassline for your tune in advance and try harmonising different bass notes. If you try a minor 7 chord and it doesn't work, try a dominant 7. As I have stressed throughout this book, the only real answer is to listen to the great jazz musicians like Joe Pass, Bill Evans and all the bass players I've mentioned, and listen closely to how they do it. Borrow (steal) their basslines and see how you can harmonise them.

Of course, there are some walking basslines that are tried and tested, which have become part of the jazz guitarist's arsenal of licks. These are a great starting point and will help to teach you what a good bassline should sound and feel like. We learn to speak a new language by using stock phrases to begin with, and the same is true in music.

In the next three chapters, I've transcribed three recordings of my playing. The first is a *rhythm changes* sequence (like *Oleo* or *I Got Rhythm*), the second is a jazz blues (such as *Blue Monk*), and the third is me playing the chord changes to *All the Things You Are* to show how this technique can be applied to any jazz standard. Each piece contains sections with one chord per bar. I want you to learn them and see how I tackle each one. You'll learn more from this than I can possibly show you by giving you hundreds of isolated options.

I've recorded two choruses of each tune, and the first time through I keep things simple. On the repeat, I throw the kitchen sink at it and go to town. Please take my ideas and analyse them to see how they work.

Good luck on the journey!

Martin and Joseph.

Chapter Eleven – Jazz Blues

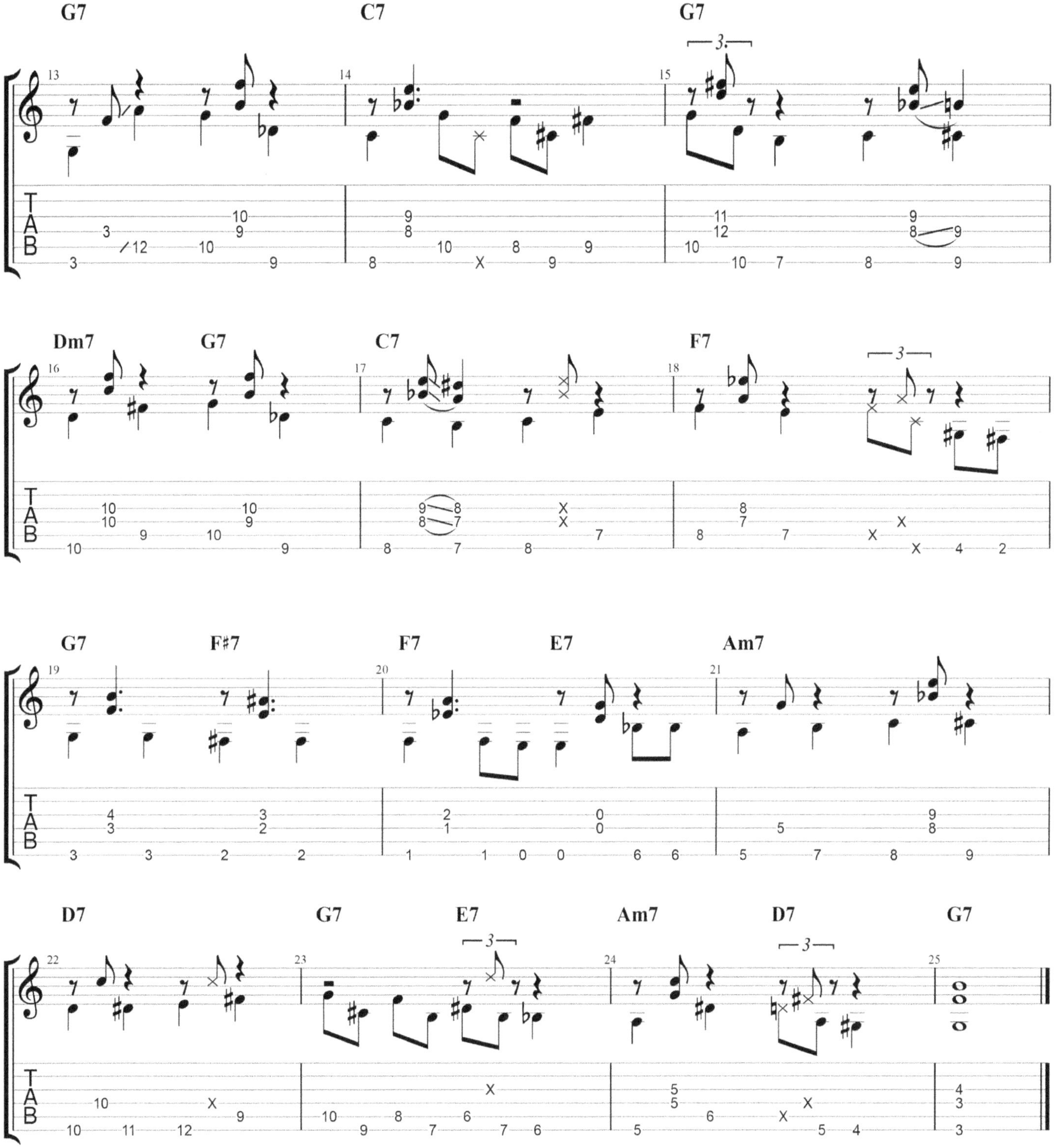
G7 C7 G7
Dm7 G7 C7 F7
G7 F#7 F7 E7 Am7
D7 G7 E7 Am7 D7 G7

Chapter Twelve – Autumn Leavers

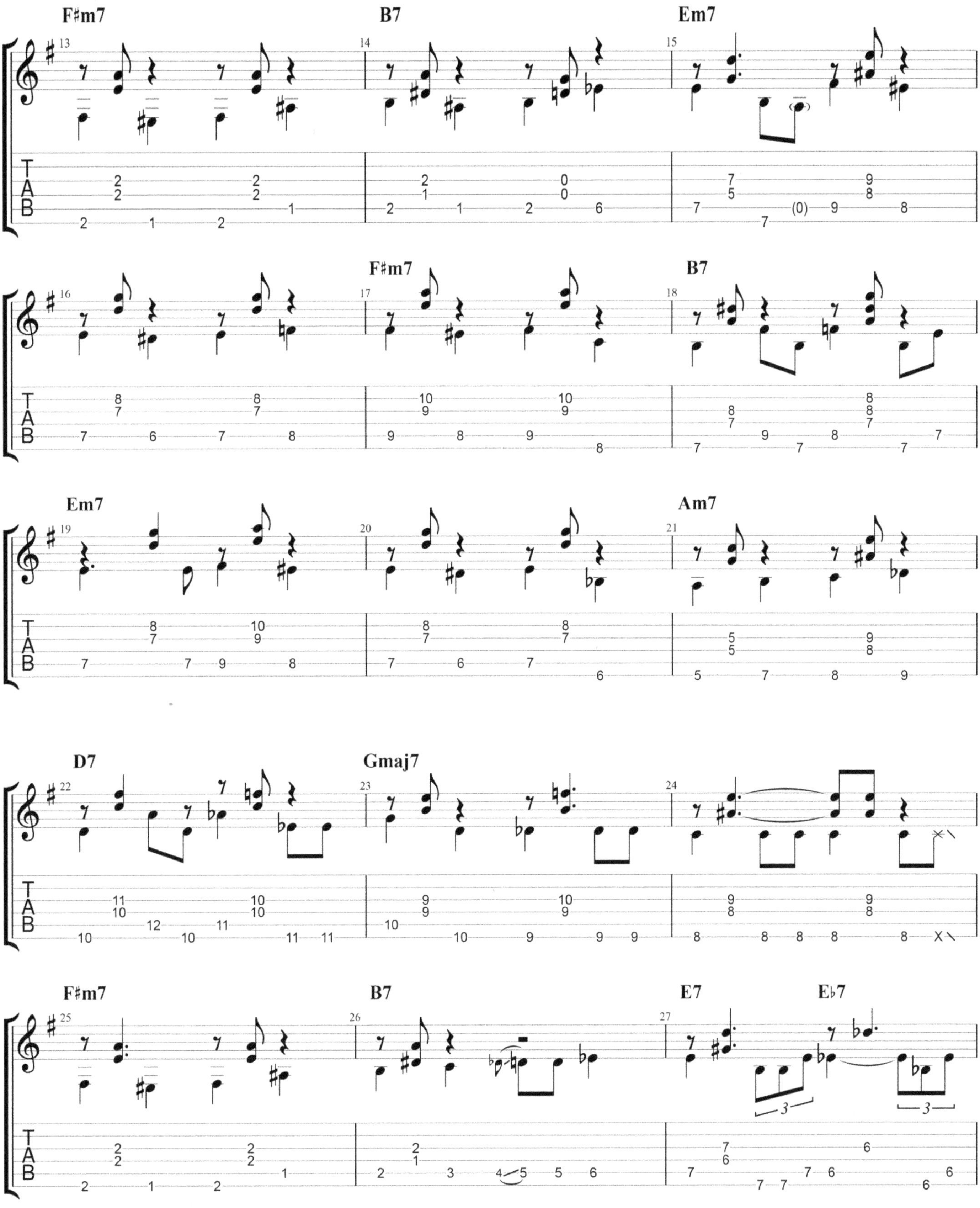
F♯m7
B7
Em7
F♯m7
B7
Em7
Am7
D7
Gmaj7
F♯m7
B7
E7
E♭7

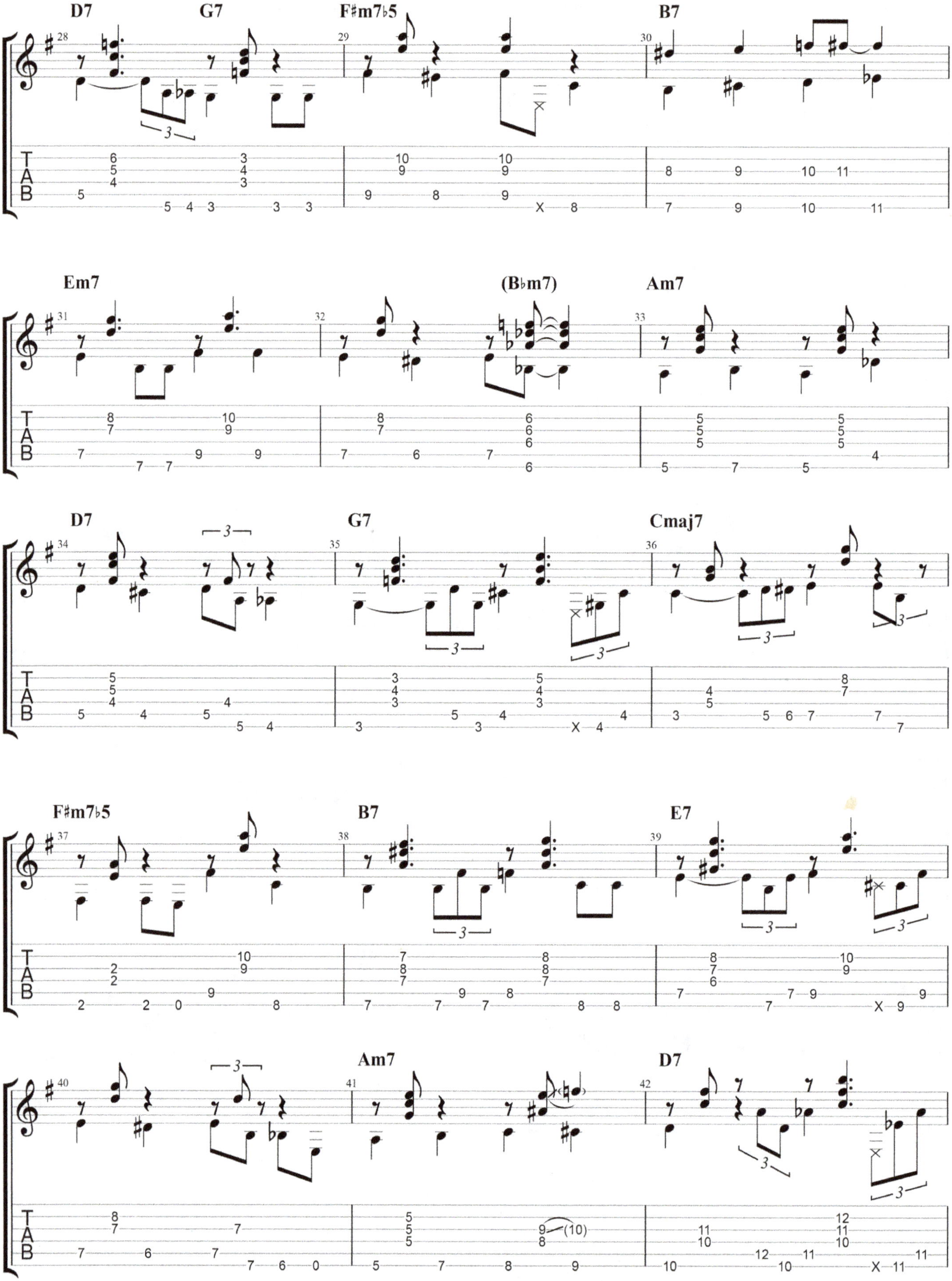
D7 G7 F#m7♭5 B7
Em7 (B♭m7) Am7
D7 G7 Cmaj7
F#m7♭5 B7 E7
Am7 D7

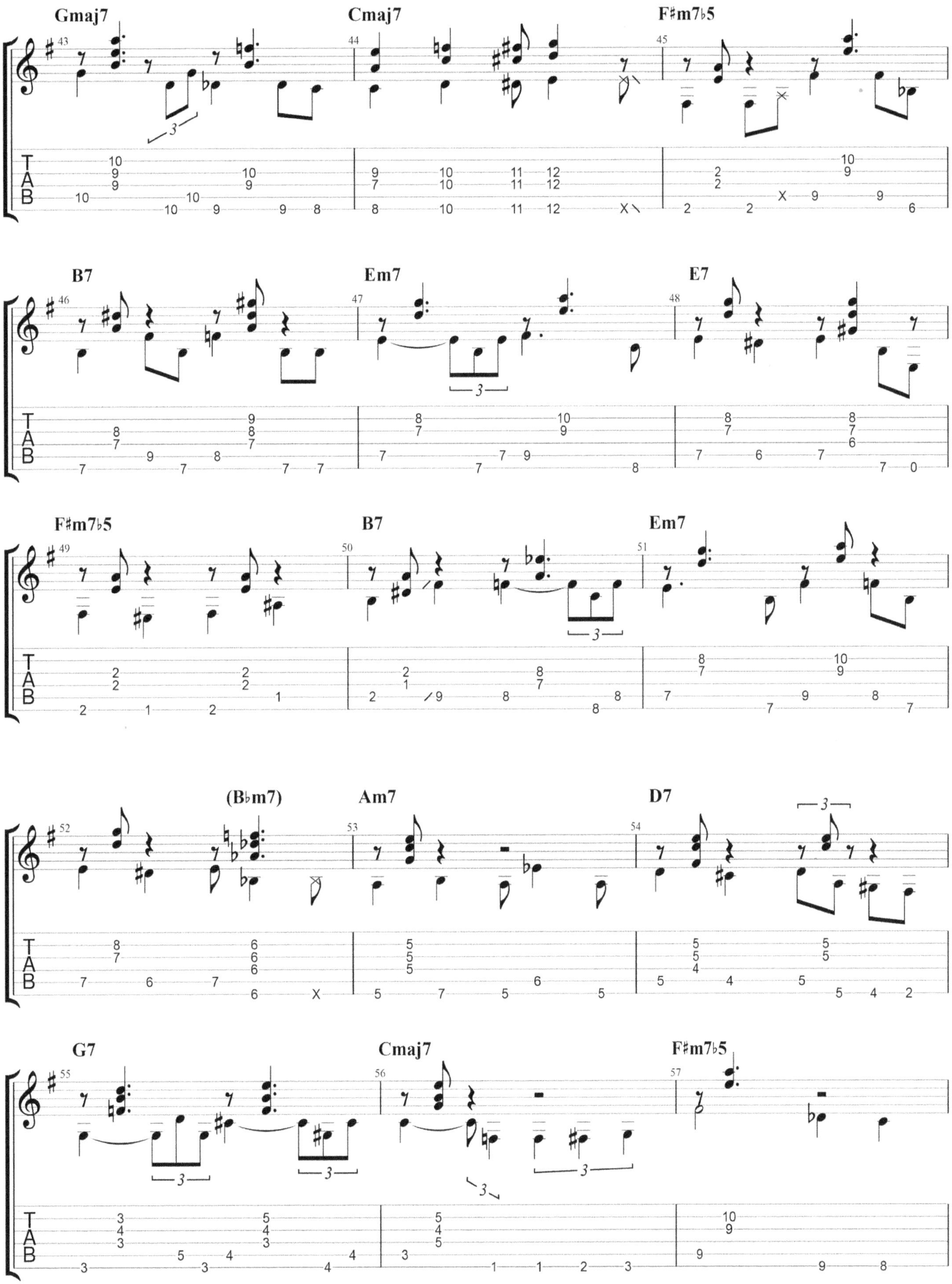
Gmaj7
Cmaj7
F♯m7♭5
B7
Em7
E7
F♯m7♭5
B7
Em7
(B♭m7)
Am7
D7
G7
Cmaj7
F♯m7♭5

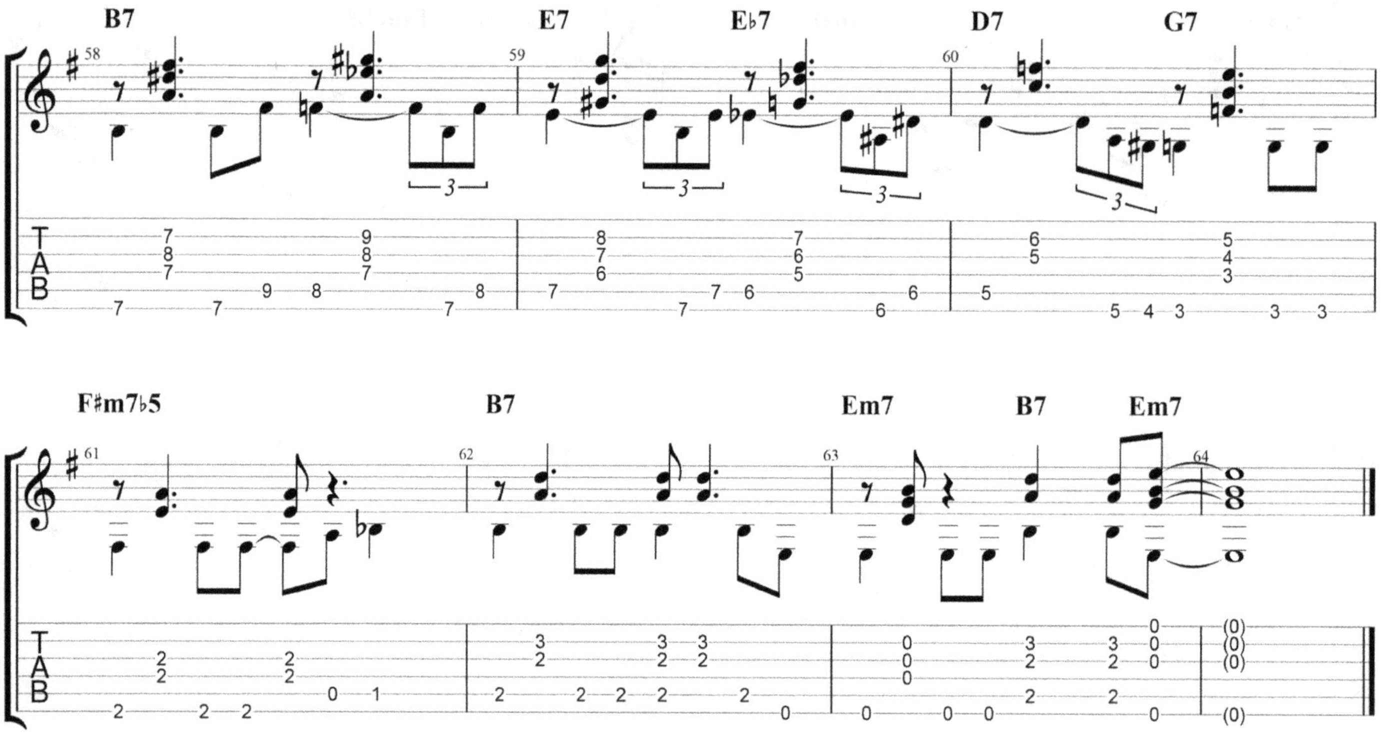
B7
E7
E♭7
D7
G7
F♯m7♭5
B7
Em7
B7
Em7

Chapter Thirteen – All The Things You Aren't

A♭7
Am7
D7
Gmaj7
Am7
B♭m7
Bm7
E7
Am7
D7
Gmaj7
Am7
B♭m7
Bm7
F♯m7♭5
B7
Emaj7
Gm7♭5
C7
Fm7
B♭m7
E♭7

A♭7 D7 D♭maj7 D♭m7 G♭7
Cm7 Bdim7 B♭m7
E♭7 Amaj7 A♭maj7 G7 C7
Fm7 B♭m7 E♭7
A♭7 D7 D♭maj7 Fm7 Dm7 G7
TAB

Cm7
Fm7
B♭7
E7
E♭maj7
A7
A♭maj7
Cm7
Am7
D7
Gmaj7
Am7
Bm7
E7
Am7
D7
Gmaj7
Am7
Bm7
G7
G♭m7♭5

B7 Emaj7 Gm7 C7
Fm7 B♭m7 E♭7
A♭maj7 D♭maj7 D♭m7 G♭7
Cm7 Bdim7 B♭m7
E♭7 A♭maj7
TAB

Conclusion and Further Listening

Well, we made it!

Congratulations on making your way through this entire book and coming out the other side unharmed. I hope it's given you a detailed understanding of how to improvise your own basslines and a real insight into the way I approach playing them on the guitar.

The next step for you is simply practice and application. Play walking basslines over your favourite tunes and use them as the basis of your own arrangements. The most important thing you can do is to listen to other musicians, particularly bass players and chord melody guitarists. Joe Pass was a great influence on me and I've borrowed a great deal of his approach in my style.

As I mentioned in the introduction, the following bass players are some of the biggest influences on my music, so please do listen to them and try to match their feel and phrasing.

• Niels-Henning Ørsted Pedersen

• Ray Brown

• Oscar Pettiford

• Jaco Pastorius

Practise without backing tracks and keep the metronome click on the 2 and the 4. This will help you to develop musical independence and great feel. It's important to be able to lay down a solid bassline without hearing any other instruments, so make sure you always know which bar you're on, and where you are in the tune.

Over time, you'll develop your own bassline "licks" that you'll be able to rely on in a tight spot. Please do steal mine and transcribe those played by the great jazz guitarists.

Finally, one overlooked part of guitar playing is the use of dynamics. Try to develop independent volume controls for each of your fingers, or at least between your fingers and thumb. By varying the volume of the different parts, you breathe new life into basslines that may otherwise sound pedestrian. Your control of dynamics really can inspire soloists and the musicians around you to better things.

Remember, you're now combining three instruments – guitar, bass and drums – the rhythmic backbone of any band. Be solid, dynamic and groovy to provide a dependable rhythm section for the other musicians.

Above all, have fun and keep exploring!

Best wishes,

Martin Taylor

Learn Jazz Guitar Chord Melody with Martin Taylor

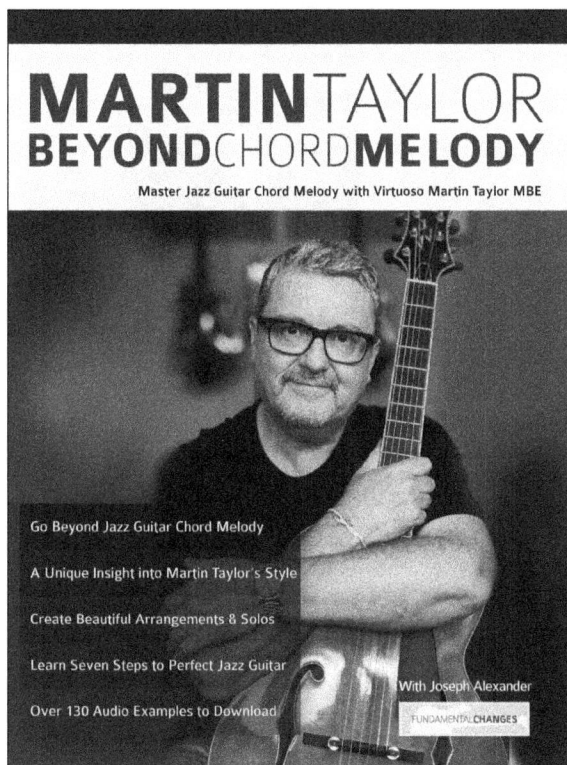

Master Jazz Guitar Chord Melody with Virtuoso Martin Taylor MBE

Beyond Chord Melody with Martin Taylor MBE condenses over 40 years of playing expertise and insight into this beautiful jazz guitar book. Learn from the internationally acclaimed master of jazz chord melody guitar as he guides you through his 7-step method to creating your own guitar arrangements. As a special bonus, two specially commissioned online videos are included, with Martin illustrating key techniques.

Putting Creative Jazz Guitar Tools in Your Hands

If you love jazz chord melody guitar, you've probably struggled to learn other people's arrangements, while struggling to create your own.

Beyond Chord Melody teaches you Martin Taylor's own secret formula for creating instant jazz guitar arrangements and gives you the tools to master your guitar and create your own stunning chord melody arrangements.

What you'll learn:

- 7 steps to jazz chord melody guitar that will unlock your creativity

- How to make a chord melody arrangement of any jazz standard.

- How to play chords and solo at the same time.

- Overcome the common blocks that stifle your progress

- Build stunning jazz chord melody guitar arrangements

- The essential components of any jazz standard

- Break away from chord boxes and discover the freedom of polyphonic guitar playing

Bonus 1: Learn a complete chord melody arrangement of an original tune to consolidate all the jazz guitar techniques and kick start your jazz chord melody guitar mastery.

Bonus 2: Two exclusive videos with Martin Taylor that clearly demonstrate the most fundamental aspects of his jazz guitar style.

Other Jazz Guitar Books from Fundamental Changes

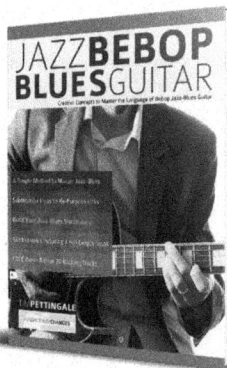

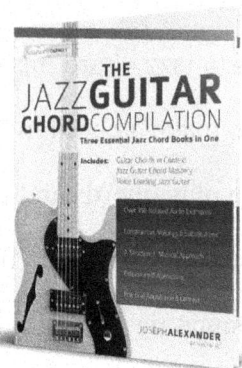

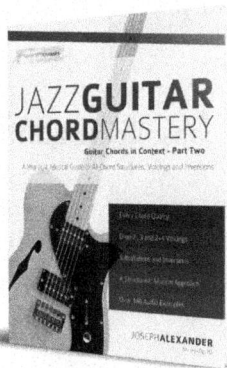

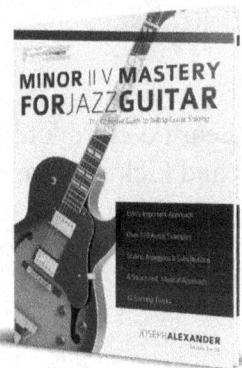

Own Martin Taylor's Joya Guitar

Own Martin's beautiful, handcrafted Joya guitar. For more information visit:

https://martintaylorguitars.com